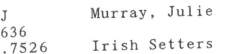

Cool

BACKYARD CAMPING

Great Things to Do in the Great Outdoors

Alex Kuskowski

Checkerboard
Library

An Imprint of Abdo Publishing
abdopublishing.com

abdopublishing.com

Published by Abdo Publishing, a division of ABDO, PO Box 398166, Minneapolis, Minnesota 55439.

Printed in the United States of America,
North Mankato, Minnesota
062015
092015

THIS BOOK CONTAINS RECYCLED MATERIALS

Content Developer: Nancy Tuminelly
Design and Production: Jen Schoeller, Mighty Media, Inc.
Series Editor: Liz Salzmann
Photo Credits: Frankie and Maclean Potts, Jen Schoeller, Shutterstock

The following manufacturers/names appearing in this book are trademarks: 3M™, Krylon® ColorMaster™, Market Pantry™, Pillsbury®, Pyrex®, Reynolds®, RITZ®, Rolo®, Rust-oleum® Painter's Touch®, Sharpie®, X-Acto®

Library of Congress Cataloging-in-Publication Data
Kuskowski, Alex.
 Cool backyard camping : great things to do in the great outdoors / Alex Kuskowski.
     pages cm. -- (Cool great outdoors)
 Includes index.
 ISBN 978-1-62403-693-4
 1. Backyard camping--Juvenile literature. I. Title.
 GV191.7.K87 2016
 796.54--dc23
                         2014045308

To Adult Helpers:

This is your chance to inspire kids to get outside! As children complete the activities in this book, they'll develop new skills and confidence. They'll even learn to love and appreciate the great outdoors!

Some of the activities in this book will require your help, but encourage kids to do as much as they can on their own. Be there to offer guidance when needed, but mostly be a cheerleader for their creative spirit and natural inspirations!

Before getting started, it helps to review the activities and set some ground rules. Remind kids that cleaning up is mandatory! Adult supervision is always recommended. So is going outside!

Key Symbols:

In this book you may see these symbols. Here is what they mean:

HOT STUFF!
This project requires the use of a stove, oven, or campfire. Always use pot holders when handling hot objects.

SHARP!
This project requires the use of a sharp object. Get help.

CONTENTS

Camp Out!

Have you ever been camping before? Do you think you have go to a state or national park to do it? Or to a big campground? Not true! You can camp in your own backyard. No backyard? No problem. Any outdoor space will do!

We spend most of our lives inside. Take a second to count the hours. You sleep inside. You eat inside. You study inside. That's life in the 21st century.

You've got to get out!

Try backyard camping. You can make great outdoor food. You can play great outdoor games! It all happens outside. And it's all good. They don't call it the great outdoors for nothing!

A NATURAL RECHARGE!

What's so great about the great outdoors? A lot! Being outside exposes us to the sun's natural light. The sun gives us **vitamin** D. Vitamin D keeps our bodies strong! Exposure to sunlight helps regulate our sleeping patterns. The more you are outside, the easier it is to fall asleep!

BACKYARD CAMPING

*H*ere are some of the things you'll need to make nature and the great outdoors your home away from home!

SHELTER

Is it warm out? Not a rain cloud in sight? Consider camping under the stars! Otherwise you'll want a tent to keep you warm and dry.

CLOTHING

Make sure you dress **appropriately**! Day and nighttime temperatures can vary greatly. Dress in layers and be prepared!

ESSENTIALS

BEDDING

Sleeping bags are **portable** beds! Some are made for extremely cold weather. Others are lighter for warmer climates. You can make a bed out of blankets too!

FOOD

You can't bring the entire refrigerator outdoors. But that doesn't mean you can't eat great food! Check out the recipes in this book for ideas!

LIGHT

If the moon is full, you can use its light when you camp. But most nights, you'll want to rely on a flashlight!

CAMPFIRE BASICS

There are products that make starting a campfire quick and easy. You can find them at most **hardware** stores and **groceries**. Or you can follow the steps on the next page. They will help you build a fire the old-fashioned way!

Why Build a Fire?

Light
Fires are useful light sources at night.

Warmth
Fires keep you and your food nice and warm in the great outdoors!

Entertainment
Fires bring people together. The best ghost stories are always told around a fire!

TRADITIONAL *Fire-Building* ESSENTIALS

FIRE PIT

Build a ring of rocks.
Or dig a pit that's
several inches deep.
This will protect
your fire.

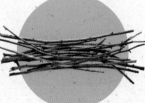

KINDLING

Dry twigs, grasses,
and paper start on fire
easily. Put them in the
fire pit first.

LOGS

Put a few logs on
the kindling. Lay
them across each
other so air can flow
between them.

FIRE STARTER

Use matches or a
lighter. Light the
kindling and blow
gently on the flame.
Soon the fire will
spread to the logs.

TYPES *of* CAMPING

If you are using a tent or a simple structure, then you are camping. But that's a pretty wide-open **definition**! There are many different ways to camp.

Backcountry Camping

Backcountry camping is camping in the middle of nowhere. You can only bring what you can carry on your back!

Backyard Camping

Backyard camping is camping in your own backyard!

ARE YOU READY?

1. Check the Weather

Check the forecast before you begin any outdoor adventure!

2. Dress Appropriately

Dress in layers! Be prepared for a **variety** of temperatures.

3. Bring Water

It's important to drink enough water, especially if it's hot out.

4. Get Permission

Some of the activities in this book require adult **supervision**. When in doubt, ask for help!

Campground Camping

Campgrounds rent out spaces for tents and motor homes. You can park right next to your spot.

Glamping

What is glamping? It's **glamorous** camping! When you go glamping, you bring all the luxuries of home with you.

Now let's get out and enjoy the great outdoors!

Materials

Here are some of the things you'll need.

3-sided foam display

acrylic coating spray

banana slices

apple slices

blueberries

blue painter's tape

box

caramels

chocolate squares

chocolate wafers

chopped walnuts

cloth-backed vinyl fabric

cookies

crescent roll dough

flashlight

foam padding

freezer paper

glow sticks

graham crackers

hole punch

hot dogs

index cards

marshmallows

measuring tape

mint chocolate

peanut butter cups

peanut butter

pen

plastic bottle

puffy paint

Ritz cracker

roasting skewers

Rolo candy

rope

ruler

scissors

spray paint

strawberry slices

tray

X-Acto knife

comfy SITTER

Make a cozy seat to rest your feet!

Materials

cloth-backed vinyl fabric,
15 × 30 inches (38 cm × 76 cm)
hole punch
foam padding
measuring tape
scissors
rope, 72 inches (183 cm)
tape

1 Fold the fabric in half to make a square. Punch holes along the three open sides. Make the holes about ½ inch (1 cm) from the edge. Space them about 1 inch (2.5 cm) apart.

2 Cut the padding to 13 by 13 inches (33 by 33 cm). Place it inside the folded vinyl fabric.

3 Wrap a piece of tape around one end of the rope. Tie a knot at the other end.

4 Push the taped end up through the two holes nearest to the fold. Pull until the knot hits the fabric. Bring the end back underneath. Push it up through the next set of holes. Continue until you've threaded the rope through all of the holes.

5 Tie a knot in the end of the rope. Cut off any extra rope.

get
GLOWING

Let glow sticks be the
light of the party!

Materials

.8-inch (20 cm) glow stick bracelets,
2 each of 5 different colors
4 empty plastic bottles
water
measuring tape

1 Crack the glow sticks. Put a different color glow stick in each plastic bottle.

2 Fill the bottles with water.

3 Make rings out of four of the remaining glow sticks. Use the ones that match the bottles.

4 Place the bottles on the ground in a row. Measure 72 inches (183 cm) away from the bottles. Use the last two glow sticks to make a line on the ground.

5 Players take turns standing behind the line. They throw the rings at the bottles. Players get one point for each ring that lands over its matching bottle. The first person with 10 points wins!

GHOST
story kit

Bring this out to liven up
the campfire group!

Materials

index cards
marker
pen
box
puffy paint
flashlight

1. Write a **category** on an index card. Choose from story elements such as characters, noises, places, animals, jobs, etc.

2. On the back of the card write at least three examples of the category.

3. Make at least twice as many cards as people. Use your imagination!

4. Decorate the box with puffy paint. Let it dry. Put the cards in the box.

5. Have everyone sit in a circle. The first person shines the flashlight under his or her chin. He or she draws two cards from the box. Then he or she begins a scary story. He or she must use one example from each card.

6. Pass the box and flashlight around. Each person draws two cards and adds to the story.

7. Continue until someone draws the last two cards. He or she must end the story.

SHADOW
puppet theater

Materials

3-sided foam display
ruler
pen
X-Acto knife
painter's tape
newspaper
spray paint
acrylic coating spray
scissors
freezer paper
colored paper
markers
craft glue
flashlight

SHARP!

1 Draw a large rectangle on the middle section of the display. Make it 18 by 14 inches (46 by 36 cm). The top should be 6 inches (15 cm) from the top of the display.

2 Carefully cut out the rectangle with an X-Acto knife.

3 Put lines of painter's tape on the front of the display. Space the lines about 3 inches (8 cm) apart.

4 Cover your work surface with newspaper. Lay the display on the newspaper. Spray paint the display. Use several light coats so the paint doesn't run. Let it dry completely after each coat.

5 Spray the display with acrylic coating to seal the paint. Use several light coats. Let it dry completely after each coat.

(continued on next page)

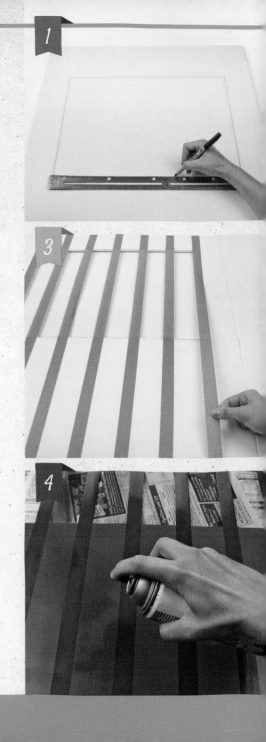

6 When completely dry, peel the painter's tape off.

7 Cut a piece of freezer paper slightly larger than the window. Lay the display face down. Put the freezer paper over the window. Place it shiny side down. Tape the freezer paper in place.

8 Decorate the display. Give your theater a name. Write it on paper. Glue it to the display. Cut out strips of paper to add a frame. Glue them around the edge of the window.

9 Set up the display outside at night. Set the light on the ground behind the display. Place it under the window. Hold your hands in front of the flashlight to create animal shapes.

TRY YOUR HAND!

*S*hadow art may have started as entertainment for cave dwellers. They created shadow stories on the cave walls. Use your hands to make the characters in your shadow theater. Try some of the shadows below. Or make up your own!

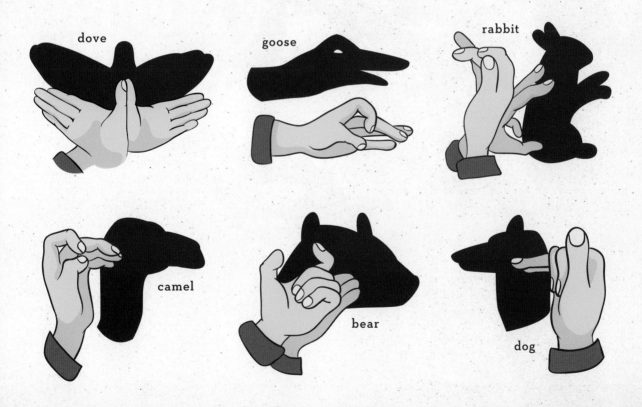

dove

goose

rabbit

camel

bear

dog

wrapped
HOT DOGS

Roast a campfire dinner!

Materials

1 can crescent roll dough
1 package hot dogs
roasting skewers
campfire
large tray

HOT!

1 Open the can of rolls. Separate the dough into triangles.

2 Put each hot dog on a roasting skewer.

3 Wrap a triangle around each hot dog. Start with the wide end of the triangle.

4 Hold a wrapped hot dog over the heat of the fire. Keep it out of the flames. Roast it until both the hot dog and the dough look cooked.

5 Set the cooked hot dogs on a tray. Let them cool slightly. Remove the skewers.

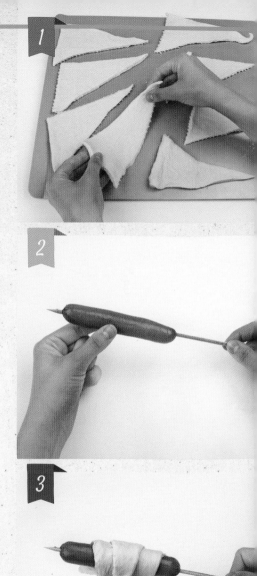

s'mores BUFFET

Make dessert the main event!

Materials

s'mores ingredients
roasting skewers
campfire

HOT!

S'mores Ingredients

The Marshmallows

- plain
- chocolate
- toasted coconut
- strawberry
- caramel

The Melty Stuff

- chocolate squares
  (milk, dark, white)
- mint chocolates
- caramels
- peanut butter cups
- Rolo candies

The Bases

- graham crackers
  (honey, chocolate, cinnamon)
- chocolate wafers
- Ritz crackers
- cookies

The Add-Ons

- banana slices
- apple slices
- strawberry slices
- blueberries
- chopped walnuts
- peanut butter

1 Choose a marshmallow, two bases, and any melty stuff or add-ons you want.

2 Set the melty stuff and add-ons on one of the bases.

3 Put the marshmallow on a skewer. Hold it over the fire. Keep it out of the flames. Turn the skewer so the marshmallow heats evenly. When the marshmallow begins to brown, it is ready.

4 Lay the marshmallow on the base that has stuff on it. Press the other base on top. Pull out the skewer. Your s'more is complete!

TRY THESE S'MORE COMBINATIONS!

The Elvis	The Grasshopper	The Caramel Apple
graham crackers	chocolate graham crackers	graham crackers
plain marshmallow	plain marshmallow	plain marshmallow
peanut butter cup	mint chocolate square	caramel candy
banana slices		apple slices

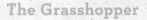

How Great Is the GREAT OUTDOORS?

*D*id you enjoy the backyard camping activities in this book? Did any of them inspire you to do more things in the great outdoors?

There is so much to love about being outside. These activities are just the beginning! Check out the other books in this series. You just might start spending more time outside than inside!

GLOSSARY

appropriately – in a manner that is suitable, fitting, or proper for a specific occasion.

category – a group of things that have something in common.

definition – the meaning of a word.

glamorous – beautiful and exciting.

grocery – a store that sells mostly food items.

hardware – metal tools and supplies used to build things.

permission – when a person in charge says it's okay to do something.

portable – easily moved or carried.

supervision – the act of watching over or directing others.

variety – different types of one thing.

vitamin – a substance needed for good health, found naturally in plants and meats.

Websites

To learn more about Cool Great Outdoors, visit **booklinks.abdopublishing.com**. These links are routinely monitored and updated to provide the most current information available.

Index